How to Make Earth-Friendly Cleaning and Beauty Supplies

Save money and save the planet by making your own time-saving organic cleaners.

Jill Heinerth

Published by:
Heinerth Productions Inc.
5989 NE County Road 340
High Springs, FL 32643 USA
First published 2014
Copyright © Jill Heinerth

Book design Heinerth Productions Inc.
www.IntoThePlanet.com
Printed in the USA
ISBN 978-1-940944-05-0

About the Author

More people have walked on the moon, than have been to some of the places that Jill's exploration has taken her right here on the earth. From the most dangerous technical dives deep inside underwater caves, to searching for never before seen ecosystems inside giant Antarctic icebergs, Jill's curiosity and passion about our watery planet is the driving force in her life.

In recognition of her lifetime achievement, Jill was awarded the inaugural Medal for Exploration. Established by the *Royal Canadian Geographical Society*, the medal recognizes singular achievements and the pursuit of excellence by an outstanding Canadian explorer.

Jill's accolades include induction as a Fellow of the *Explorer's Club* and the inaugural class of the *Women Diver's Hall of Fame*. She received the Wyland ICON Award, an honor she shares with several of her underwater heroes including Jacques Cousteau, Robert Ballard and Dr. Sylvia Earle. She was named a "Living Legend" by *Sport Diver Magazine* and selected as *Scuba Diving Magazine's* "Sea Hero of the Year."

With her project, the "*We Are Water Project*", she has produced a documentary film, live speaking tour, art exhibits and interactive web resources to lead an educational effort to help people make everyday behavioral changes that foster greater access to and preservation of our endangered fresh water resources.

In support of this effort, Jill and her husband Robert McClellan rode their bicycles 4,300 miles across Canada, from British Columbia to Newfoundland in 2013, meeting people and through presentations to groups large and small, spread the message of "water literacy." Her website www.IntoThePlanet.com provides links to her exploration and water advocacy efforts.

WE ARE WATER

www.WeAreWaterProject.com

Introduction

I am a cave diver. I swim through the veins of Mother Earth, exploring the shadowy recesses inside our planet. The foreboding doorways of underwater caves repel most people, but I am attracted to the constricted corridors, pressing my way through the blackness while relying on sophisticated technology for each sustaining breath. This is my workplace. Within the darkness of my office, survival depends on subsuming both curiosity and fear.

I work with biologists discovering new species, physicists tracking climate change and hydrogeologists examining our finite freshwater reserves. Following the course of water where ever it guides me, my exploration has allowed me to witness new life forms inside Antarctic icebergs, skeletal remains of ancient civilizations and geologic formations that tell the story of earth's past.

Underwater caves are museums of natural history, that teach us about evolution and survival. They are portals to the mythic underworld of indigenous cultures and windows to the aquifer from which we drink. As I swim through these caverns measureless to man, it is not my own survival that I dwell on, but the survival of our water planet.

Sometimes I fear that we will not rise to meet the challenges of our current global environmental and social crises. Then, I meet a young girl who wants to make the world a better place. My optimism expands.

There is plenty of water on our big blue planet, but we are running out of clean freshwater we can afford. We all need to know where our water comes from, how we pollute it and how we can protect it for the future generations. We have to protect it from corporate interests whose success relies on commodifying and selling it to the highest bidder. Clean water is not just our greatest treasure, it is a basic human right. Helping young minds understand and embrace their water planet is key to our survival. We are water.

I'm a student of this planet and have been learning to tread as lightly as possible. I want the things I put in my body and in my house to be as simple and clean as possible. My parent's generation created a world of convenience, but that often required new chemicals and compounds that weren't good for us. This book is a compilation of all my favorite recipes for everyday household cleaning and beauty items. It will help you simplify life and get back to basics, passed down from the wisdom of our grandmothers. The cool part is that it will make your house safer, protect the planet and save you time and money too.

Table of Contents

The Basic Pantry

There are a few basic items you should stock in your pantry in order to make earth-friendly cleaning supplies. Many of these items can be used alone or can be combined with other items in the recipes that follow.

Note: These formulas and substitutions are offered to help minimize the use of toxic substances in your home, and reduce the environmental harm caused by the manufacture, use and disposal of toxic chemicals and compounds. Results may vary and cannot be guaranteed to be 100% safe and effective. Before applying any cleaning or beauty formulations, test in small hidden areas if possible. Always use caution with any new product in your home.

Baking Soda
Basic pH 9

Baking soda has proven virus-killing abilities. It will also clean, deodorize, brighten and cut through grease.

Castille Soap
Basic pH 8.9

Castille soap is made from plant oils. No animal products or chemical detergents are added. The most popular brand is Dr. Bronner's. This soap cuts through grease well.

White Vinegar
Acid pH 2.4

Vinegar is acidic and eliminates grease, soap scum, and grime.

Lemons
Acid pH 2

Natural lemon juice will eliminate mildew and mold in addition to smelling fresh. It is also a good grease cutter and will shine hard surfaces.

Olive Oil
Olive oil works as a cleaner and polisher in addition to being a great cooking oil.

Essential Oils
Essential oils are 100% natural plant compounds that can be used to scent your homemade cleaning products. The strong scents can trigger allergies in some people, so use sparingly and choose a scent that works for you. Some oils are also antibacterial, including lavender, tea tree, and rosemary.

Borax
Basic pH 9.3

Many generations have been using borax as a household cleaner. It is a mineral called sodium borate. Powdered borax is white, consisting of soft colorless crystals that dissolve easily in water. Borax first came into common use in the late 19th century in the American west since it was cheaply mined in the California and Nevada deserts. It was sold as "2o Mule Team Borax." It cleans, deodorizes, disinfects, softens water, cleans wallpaper, painted walls and floors.

Apple Cider Vinegar
Acid pH 4.25-5

Organic apple cider vinegar is antibacterial, antiviral and antifungal, so it can soothe your sore throat, remove a wart and clean your vegetables.

Vegetable Glycerine
Commonly made of palm or coconut oil, glycerin is a popular additive to soaps and cleansers for dry skin because of its lubricating properties.

Rubbing Alcohol
pH 5.5

Easy to find at a grocery or drug store, rubbing alcohol is a staple for your cleaning and first aid cabinet.

Washing Soda
Washing soda is sodium carbonate decahydrate, a mineral. Washing soda cuts grease, removes stains, softens water, cleans wall, tiles, sinks and tubs. Use with care, since washing soda can irritate mucous membranes. Do not use on aluminum.

Cornstarch
Cornstarch can be used to clean windows, polish furniture, shampoo carpets and rugs.

Microfiber Cloths

These cloths lift off dirt, grease and dust without the need for cleaning chemicals, because they are formulated to penetrate and trap dirt. There are a number of different brands and a good quality cloth can last for several years. Otherwise, use old clothing cut into rags for most applications of cleaning products.

Cellulose Sponges

Most household sponges are made of polyester or plastic which are slow to break down in landfills, and many are treated with triclosan, a chemical that can produce chloroform (a suspected carcinogen) when it interacts with the chlorine found in tap water. Instead try cellulose sponges, available at natural foods stores, which are biodegradable and will soak up spills faster since they're naturally more absorbent.

Simple Chemistry

Most of these ingredients can combined; however some products can essentially cancel each other out since some are basic or alkaline and some are acid. However, you can still wash with a base, like castille soap, and rinse with an acid, such as vinegar.

All Purpose Cleaners

All Purpose Hard Surface Cleaner

- 2 cups of white, distilled vinegar
- 2 cups water
- up to 20-30 drops of antibacterial essential oil (lavender, tea tree, rosemary, etc.)

This cleaner can be used for counters, floors, windows and mirrors. Mix ingredients in a spray bottle for easy dispensing. If the dirt is tough, heat the mixture in a glass container.

If your countertop is granite or marble, replace the vinegar with rubbing alcohol since it is less acidic.

Soft Scrubber

- 2 cups of baking soda
- ½ cup castille soap
- 4 teaspoons of vegetable glycerine
- 6 drops of antibacterial essential oil (lavender, tea tree, rosemary, etc.)

Mix together until it resembles cake icing – if it is too thick, add more liquid soap. Store in a sealed glass jar for up to 2 years. This scrub is useful for kitchen counters, stove tops, ceramic sinks, shower tiles, etc.

Window Cleaner

- ¼ - ½ tsp of castille soap
- ¼ cup of vinegar
- 2 cups of water

Put all ingredients in a spray bottle. Shake the mixture up and use a lint free cloth or old newspaper to apply. Add lemon for scent and extra grease cutting power.

Wood Polish

- ½ tsp of olive oil
- ¼ cup vinegar or fresh lemon juice

Mix ingredients in a glass jar. Dab a soft rag into the solution and wipe onto wood surfaces. Cover the glass jar when not in use – store forever.

Cleansing Wood Polish

- ¼ cup of vinegar or fresh lemon juice
- ¾ cup of olive oil

Mix ingredients in a glass jar. Dab a soft rag into the solution and wipe onto wood surfaces. Cover the glass jar when not in use – store forever.

Disinfectant Spray

- 2 cups water
- 3 tbsp. castille soap
- 20-30 drops of tea tree oil

Mix in a spray bottle and use as needed.

Air Freshener

- Glass Mason Jar
- Baking soda
- 5 drops essential oil
- Small piece of card stock

Fill a glass mason jason ¼ full with baking soda. Add five drops of your favorite smelling essential oil. Take inner lid of mason jar and use it to trace a circle on a small piece of lightweight cardboard. Cut out the circle and poke small holes in it with a thumbtack. Use mason jar ring to secure this on the jar. Alternately, reuse an old salt shaker to do the same job.

Bathroom

Foaming Hand Soap

- Reuse a foaming hand soap dispenser
- Fill 1/5th of container with liquid castille soap
- Top with water
- Add 2 drops of tea tree oil
- Add 2 drops of essential oil if you want it scented
- Shake to mix ingredients

Toilet Cleaner

- Baking soda – sprinkle into toilet bowl
- Lemon juice – spray onto bowl after sprinkling baking soda

Let the mixture stand while you clean the rest of the bathroom. Scrub with a toilet bowl brush. Flush to rinse.

To clean your toilet rim and rest of porcelain, spray straight white vinegar and wipe clean. Add a few drops of essential oil for a nice smell.

Heavy Duty Toilet Cleaner

- ½ cup baking soda - pour into bowl
- add 10 drops tea tree oil into the bowl
- add ¼ cup of vinegar

Scrub with a toilet brush as the mixture fizzes.

Tub and Shower Mildew Cleaner

Spray pure white vinegar on mold and mildew. Let stand for 30 minutes then rinse or wipe with sponge.

Daily Soap Scum Shower Spray

- 1 cup water
- 1 cup white vinegar
- 4 drops essential oil

Mix in a spray bottle. Spray after showering. Let stand for three minutes. Wipe away.

Laundry Room

Laundry Soap

- 1 bar castille soap
- 1 cup of borax powder
- 1 cup of washing soda (Arm & Hammer is a common brand)

Grate the bar of non-toxic bar soap into a bowl with a cheese grater. Add the borax powder and washing soda. Mix in the bowl and transfer to a glass container for storage. This recipe is very concentrated so use only 1 tbsp. per load or 2-3 tbsp. for heavily soiled loads. Add ½ cup of vinegar to rinse cycle to remove soap residue and whiten your whites.

Fabric Softener

- one gallon white vinegar
- 20-30 drops essential oil

Shake jug before using each time. Add 1/3 cup to each laundry load.

Laundry Soap Nuts

Soapberries are a completely natural product. When you bounce them around in the washing machine, they release natural saponin which helps water dissolve dirt and stains from your clothing. Toss them in the machine whole, put them in a small cotton bag, grind them up or dissolve them in hot water. You can use 6 or 7 soap nuts for several loads and add a little essential oil to make the laundry smell fresh. When they are spent, simply compost them in the garden.

Laundry Bleach

Add lemon juice to the rinse cycle.

Kitchen

All Purpose Hard Surface Cleaner

- 2 cups of white, distilled vinegar
- 2 cups water
- up to 20-30 drops of antibacterial essential oil (lavender, tea tree, rosemary, etc.)

This cleaner can be used for counters, floors, windows and mirrors. Mix ingredients in a spray bottle for easy dispensing. If the dirt is tough, heat the mixture in a glass container.

If your countertop is granite or marble, replace the vinegar with rubbing alcohol since it is less acidic.

Cutting Board Cleaner

Use ½ lemon and rub over surface to disinfect. Add salt if you need scrubbing power.

Oven Cleaner

Heat oven to 250°F and spray "All Purpose Hard Surface Cleaner" on baked on grime. Pour salt on the worst areas. Let the oven cool and scrub with a sponge. If you still have trouble areas, use baking soda instead of salt.

Microwave Cleaner

- ½ cup vinegar
- 1 tbsp. lemon juice

Place ingredients in glass jar or cup. Run the microwave for 2 minutes. Leave door closed for five minutes. Open and wipe the surfaces clean. No scrubbing required. If you have let the oven get crusty, use baking soda as a scrubber.

Garbage Disposal Cleaner

Fill an ice cube tray with 1 cup of vinegar and top with water. Freeze. Toss a few cubes in garbage disposal and run as usual.

Septic Safe Drain Cleaner

- 2 cups boiling water
- ½ cup baking soda

Pour baking soda into drain and follow it with water. If this does not work then follow the baking soda with ½ cup vinegar. Cover the drain tightly with stopper or lid of pot. Allow the mixture to fizz. When it slows down add 2 cups of boiling water.

Pan Scrubber

Sprinkle dry salt and scrub.

Cast Iron Pan Scrubber

Scrub with a splash of olive oil and a tsp. of coarse salt then rinse with hot water and re-apply oil.

Non Toxic Silver Cleaner

Line your sink or a bucket with aluminum foil. Lay out silver items on the foil. Fill with boiling water. Add one cup of baking soda and a pinch of salt. Allow the silver to sit for several minutes until the tarnish disappears.

Magic Metal Cleaners

Aluminum
Using a soft cloth to rub clean with a mixture of cream of tartar and water.

Brass or Bronze
Polish with a soft cloth dipped in lemon and baking-soda solution, or vinegar and salt solution. Another method is to apply a dab of ketchup on a soft cloth and rub over tarnished spots.

Chrome
Polish with olive oil, vinegar, or aluminum foil with the shiny side out.

Copper
Soak a cotton rag in a pot of boiling water with 1 tablespoon salt and 1 cup white vinegar. Apply to copper while hot; let cool, then wipe clean. For tougher jobs, sprinkle baking soda or lemon juice on a soft cloth, then wipe. For copper cookware, sprinkle a lemon wedge with salt, then scrub. A simpler method

is to apply a dab of ketchup on a soft cloth and rub over tarnished spots.

Gold

Clean with organic toothpaste, or a paste of salt, vinegar, and flour.

Stainless Steel

Clean with a cloth dampened with undiluted white vinegar, or olive oil. For stainless cookware, mix 4 tbsp. baking soda in 4 cups of water, and apply using a soft cloth. Wipe dry using a clean cloth. For stainless steel sinks, pour some club soda on an absorbent cloth to clean, then wipe dry using a clean cloth.

Dishwasher Duet

- 1 cup castille soap
- 1 cup water
- 2 tsp. lemon juice

Mix ingredients in a glass jar. Use in first compartment of dishwasher. Fill second compartment with white vinegar.

Dish Soap

- 1 cup castille soap
- 3 tbsp. water
- 2-3 drops essential oil for scent

Shake well and store indefinitely.

Fridge Freshener

- ½ cup baking soda
- bucket of hot water

Wipe down the walls and shelves with a sponge or rag.

Safe Disinfectant "Bleach"

- ½ cup baking soda
- 1 tsp. castille soap
- ½ cup baking soda
- ½ tsp. hydrogen peroxide

Use a cloth to apply, scrub, then rinse clean.

Veggie Wash

- ½ cup apple cider vinegar
- ½ cup water
- 1 tsp. hydrogen peroxide

Mix together in a spray bottle. Use to wash veggies or meat to clean away parasites, molds and pesticides.

Kitchen Odor Neutralizer

If you are having a party and the garlic, onion and fish smells are overwhelming, boil a saucepan containing a solution of 1 tablespoon of apple cider vinegar and 1 cup of water to neutralize smells. Apple cider vinegar will also remove smells from your hands.

Around the House

Floor Cleaner and Polish

Tile Floors

Mix 2 cups vinegar in 4 cups of warm water. Use a mop or rag and don't rinse off.

Vinyl and Linoleum

Mix 1 cup vinegar and a few drops of essential oil in 1 gallon warm water. For tough jobs, add 1/4 cup borax. Use sparingly on lineoleum.

Wood

Apply a thin coat of 1:1 vegetable oil and vinegar and rub in well.

Painted Wood

Mix 1 teaspoon washing soda into 1 gallon hot water.

Walls

- ¼ cup of vinegar
- 4 cups of warm water

Wipe down walls with a rag. Scrub any black marks with baking soda on a sponge.

Hornet Deterrent

- ½ oz. citronella oil
- ⅛ oz. pennyroyal oil
- ¼ oz. lavender oil
- ⅛ oz. tea tree oil
- ⅛ oz. jojoba oil

Mix ingredients in a spray bottle. Spray the mixture around the yard, on outdoor furniture, and even on clothing to deter hornets and wasps.

Hornet Decoy

Hang a large paperbag stuffed with newspaper in an area where you want to deter hornets. Tie the top of the bag with twine. Since it resembles a nest, hornets see this and move on to occupy another space.

Mole Deterrent

- ½ cup castor oil
- 2 gallons of water

Pour over mole hills in your yard. It won't kill them, but they will relocate.

Natural Weed Killer

Pure vinegar in a spray bottle acts like Mother Nature's "Round-Up" spray. It kills everything that is sprayed.

Homemade Disinfecting Wipes

- 1 cup water
- 2 tbsp. white vinegar
- ½ tbsp. castille soap
- 8-10 drops lemon essential oil or tea tree oil

Mix ingredients together and pour over a small recloseable container filled with cut rags from old shirts, microfiber clothes or other cotton fabrics. Wash and reuse.

Hangover House Fixer

To eliminate the smell of cigarette smoke, spilled beer, vomit, paint or other strong smells from a room simply place a bowl of apple cider vinegar on the floor overnight. You can do the same for vehicles, sheds, refrigerators and coolers.

Mothballs

Aromatic cedar wood (sometimes called juniper) or cedar oil in an absorbent cloth will repel moths. Homemade moth-repelling sachets can be made with lavender, rosemary, and rose petals. Dried lemon peels are also a natural moth deterrent - simply toss into clothes chest, or tie in cheesecloth and hang in the closet.

Beauty Aids

Arthritis Pain Rub

Relieve achy joints with a paste of castor oil and turmeric or cayenne powder. Do not get this in your eyes as it will irritate.

Bug Repellent

Pure pennyroyal (mint) or citronella oil will repel most insects including mosquitoes. If you apply directly to your skin, try a small test patch first. Some people react to strong essential oils. Citronella may stain clothes.

Callus and Corn Treatment

- ½ cup castor oil
- 6 drops tea tree oil

Massage in to corns, calluses and rough spots. It will help alleviate swelling and pain and soften skin over time.

Dandruff Remover

- ¼ cup apple cider vinegar
- ¼ cup water

Mix together in a spray bottle. Spray into hair after shampooing and let sit for 15 minutes then rinse. Use twice per week. The acidity in the vinegar makes it more difficult for the fungus that contributes to dandruff to grow on the scalp.

Exfoliator

Use the recipe for the facial scrub below or simply mix equal parts of olive or coconut oil and sugar. For degreasing hands and really messy clean ups, exfoliate with baking soda and castille soap and rinse.

Facial Moisturizer

Pure coconut oil is full of collagen supporting lauric acid and anti-bacterial properties and is easily absorbed by your skin.

Facial Scrub

- 1 cup sugar
- ½ cup almond oil (olive oil or coconut oil is fine too)
- ½ tsp. Vitamin E oil (squeeze a couple of capsules)
- ½ tsp. real vanilla extract
- 15 drops of lavender essential oil

Mix together and store in wide mouth glass jar. Use as facial or hand scrub.

Foot Freshener

- 1 cup of apple cider vinegar

Pour over organic baby wipes or homemade cotton rags in a tupperware container. The acids in the apple cider vinegar alters the pH of your skin and fight off bacteria that cause smelly feet. This can also be sprayed in troublesome shoes.

Skin Cleanser

Use diluted apple cider vinegar on your skin with a wash cloth. The apple cider vinegar absorbs oils and reduces fine lines as well as restoring the proper pH to your skin. Over night, it will reduce age spots, pimples and acne scars.

Skin Smoother

- ½ oz. apple cider vinegar
- 3 oz. mineral water
- 5 plain aspirin tablets, uncoated

Crush aspirin tablets and add with apple cider vinegar and water. Store in refrigerator for cooling exfoliator scrub that will brighten complexion and smooth bumpy dry skin or acne scars.

Stretch Mark and Scar Treatment

Castor oil rubbed into the skin is a great general health care treatment and especially good for improving elasticity of skin, lessening scars and preventing stretch marks in pregnancy.

Toe Nail Fungus Remover

- 1 tsp. of tea tree oil
- ½ tsp. of olive oil
- Cotton balls

Soak cotton ball with oils and apply to nail, leaving it on to dry naturally. Do this every morning and evening until nail fungus is gone.

Toe Nail Fungus Foot Soaks

- 4-5 tbsp. of baking soda
- 1 cup of apple cider vinegar
- Warm water

Mix the vinegar with warm water and soak for 15 minutes. Then add the baking soak and soak for 15 minutes more. The vinegar kills the fungus and baking soda inhibits the growth of more. Do this twice daily until the fungus is gone.

Toe Nail Fungus Cream

Rub coconut oil onto the affected nail(s). Wash hands well. Do this 2-3 times per day until nail fungus is gone. The fatty acids in the coconut oil insert themselves into the fat layer of the fungal membrane and it break down the fungus which will disappear over time.

Tooth Whitener

Use a Q-tip to apply apple cider vinegar on teeth occasionally. Rinse. Do not do this too often since the acid can damage enamel. A gentler deodorizing mouthwash can be made with one tsp. of apple cider vinegar in water.

Youthful Eyes

Before bed, rub castor oil around our eyes. It will soak in overnight, leaving you more youthful and refreshed looking in the morning.

Stain Guide

Carpet Stains

Mix equal parts white vinegar and water in a spray bottle. Spray directly on stain, let sit for several minutes, and clean with a brush or sponge using warm soapy water.

For fresh grease spots, sprinkle corn starch onto spot and wait 15 - 30 minutes before vacuuming.

For a heavy duty carpet cleaner, mix ¼ cup each of salt, borax and vinegar. Rub paste into carpet and let stand for a few hours. Vacuum.

Coffee and Tea Stains

Stains in cups can be removed by applying vinegar to a sponge and wiping. Baking soda will cut through tougher scale.

To clean a teakettle or coffee maker, add 2 cups water and ¼ cup vinegar; bring to a boil. Let cool, wipe with a clean cloth and rinse thoroughly with water.

Lime and Scale Deposits

To remove lime scale on bathroom fixtures, squeeze real lemon juice onto scale and let rest for several minutes before wiping clean with a wet cloth or use 2 cups of warm water with ¼ cup vinegar in same way.

Rust Remover

Sprinkle a little salt on the rust, squeeze a lime over the salt until it is well soaked. Leave the mixture on for 2 - 3 hours. Use leftover lime rind to scrub residue.

Stickers

To remove, sponge vinegar over them several times, and wait 15 minutes, then rub off the stickers. This also works for price tags (stickers) on tools, etc.

Wallpaper Remover

Mix equal parts of white vinegar and hot water, apply with sponge over the old wallpaper to soften the adhesive. Peel off by lifting the paper and reapply the mixture to stubborn patches. Open the room windows or use a fan to dissipate the vinegar or add peppermint essential oil to freshen the smell.

Pet Stains

For fresh urine stains on carpet, soak up as much liquid as possible, then sprinkle the area with baking soda. Allow it to sit until the baking soda has soaked up all of the moisture, then vacuum. For urine or vomit stains on hard surfaces, scrub the area with coarse salt or baking soda. Rinse the area with club soda and dry it. Organic milk can help loosen dried blood stains and organic toothpaste makes an effective scrub for tougher stains on hard surfaces.

Homemade OxyClean

- 2 cups water
- 1 cup hydrogen peroxide
- 1 cup washing soda

Mix together and use in spray bottle or store in glass jar.

We Are Water

Water composes approximately 70% of the human body.
It also makes up 70% of our planet.
Access to clean water helps assure a more just,
secure and sustainable world.

For the first time in history, fresh water has become a finite resource. Many experts agree that, without significant changes in water policy, wars of the 21st century may be fought, not over oil, but for control of clean water.

There is no doubt that everything we do to the surface of the earth will eventually soak into the ground and be returned to us to drink. It is a frightening future that lays ahead, but we can all make positive changes in our life to improve the health and abundance of clean water on earth.

To learn more, please visit: WeAreWaterProject.com.

Things You Can Do To Save Water

In the Bathroom

- Turn off water while brushing teeth - save 360 liters per week.
- Fix a dripping tap - save 300 gallons per year.
- Reduce shower from seven to four minutes - save 60 liters each time.
- Install low flow shower head - save 11 liters per minute, 750 gallons/month.
- Install dual flush toilet - save 50% each flush.
- Put a plug in basin while shaving - 9 liters per minute.
- Capture shower water for the garden.
- Flush less - save 2 to 7 gallons each time.
- Put a brick in the toilet tank - save a liter each flush.
- Turn off water while you shampoo and condition your hair - save 50 gallons a week.
- Pee while you shower!

In the Kitchen

- Turn off water while cleaning up the kitchen - save 100 gallons per week.
- Buy a water efficient dishwasher - save 50% each time.
- Only wash a full load of dishes - save 120 gallons per month.
- Use economy setting on dishwasher - save 4 liters.
- Compost instead of using your garbage disposal - save 9 liters per minute.
- Catch and use running water while it warms up.
- Plug the sink to rinse dishes or veggies.

- Defrost the night before in your fridge instead of using running water .
- Use a wash basin in sink, then recycle water to the garden.
- Fix a drip - save up to 75 liters a day.
- Save cold water in the fridge instead of running the tap.
- Become a part time vegetarian.
- Eat less meat.
- Install a low flow faucet - save 50% of your water use.
- Buy WaterSense appliances.
- Use veggie rinse water on plants.
- Reuse the same drinking glass all day.
- Soak and scrape pots and pans rather than running water.
- Reuse veggie cooking water for tasty soup stock.

In the Laundry
- Use a water efficient washing machine - save 30 gallons every load.
- Only wash a full load of laundry - saves 10 liters.
- Consider installing a grey water system to recycle laundry water.
- Pretreat stains so they only get washed once.
- Buy EnergyStar appliances.
- Use natural soap nuts instead of detergent.
- Attach a hose to your washing machine outlet pipe for use in the garden.

Around the House
- Use old fish tank water on plants.
- Teach kids to turn off faucets properly.

- Reduce the distance from the water heater to the sink.
- Try on-demand water heaters for the shower or kitchen.
- Insulate hot water pipes to retain heat.
- Look for EPA WaterSense labels.
- Drink tap water.
- Avoid putting medications in the toilet.
- Avoid putting chemicals in the toilet or down the sink.
- Route the air conditioner outlet pipe to somewhere you need water in the garden.
- Don't put fat and grease down the sink. Mix it with bird seeds and invite birds to your garden.
- Buy a used car. It takes 120,000 gallons of water to make a new one.
- Reuse clothing. It takes 1800 gallons to make a pair of blue jeans.
- Drive less. It takes 70 gallons of water to produce one gallon of gas.
- Give $15 to CharityWater.org so someone in the developing world can have a clean water supply.
- Ride your bicycle instead of driving.
- Think before you buy. Is there something you can recycle or reuse?

Outside

- Irrigate early or late but not in the sunny part of the day.
- Avoid irrigating on windy days.
- Use less fertilizer.

- Create more shade in your yard to retain moisture in your plants and lawn.
- Use rain barrels.
- Eliminate herbicides.
- Pull weeds instead of using RoundUp.
- Replace part of the lawn with pebbles.
- Plants more shrubs.
- Mulch and compost your garden.
- Use old blankets, carpet or cardboard in between crop rows for weed barriers.
- Group veggies in your garden by water needs.
- Mulch the garden to reduce evaporation - reduces watering 70%.
- Aerate and spike lawns in the spring for deep roots and drought tolerance.
- Check the pool for leaks - save 500 liters per day.
- Cover the pool or hot tub (or just get rid of it).
- Don't trim the grass too short - longer needs less water.
- Plant drought resistant native plants.
- Direct rain gutters to plants that need it.
- Pee in the yard.
- Cover rain barrels.
- If you irrigate on a timer, install a rain shutoff.
- Pee in your compost pile.
- Direct the air conditioner drips to plants that need it.
- If you have to water, use drip irrigation.
- Check outdoor taps for leaks - save 1000 liters per year.
- Water the garden with a trigger nozzle not a sprinkler.
- Use a bucket and sponge to wash the car.

- Go to a car wash that reuses water.
- Wash your car on the lawn.
- Wash your car while it's raining.
- Collect rainwater for the garden.
- Sweep the driveway instead of hosing it down.
- Look for leaks - check water meter for two hours during no consumption period.
- Add walkway pavers and patio areas and let them runoff to garden.
- Plant more shrubs and ground cover to reduce the lawn.
- Water plants deeply but less often to improve drought tolerance.
- Learn where your master water shutoff valve is located.
- Let your lawn go dormant.
- Wash the dog on the grass.

In Your School

- Report leaking taps and toilets to teachers - save 300 gallons.
- Nominate a water monitor to look for leaks.
- Put up posters to remind each other to turn off taps.
- Wash art supplies in a recycled ice cream container.
- Learn how to monitor the water meter.
- Ask your science teacher to help locate your watershed.
- Use less paper.

At the Office

- Wash dishes once at the end of the day.
- Appoint a daily dish washer.
- Upgrade to dual flush toilets.

- Talk about water conservation measures in staff meetings.
- Use less paper.
- Determine if there is a way to reuse water at your business.
- Conduct a water audit of your company.
- Use a refillable water bottle for drinking.

While You Travel
- Reuse the hotel towels.
- Drink tap water.

www.ingramcontent.com/pod-product-compliance
Lightning Source LLC
Chambersburg PA
CBHW021339290326
41933CB00038B/978